HENRI DE TOULOUSE-LAUTREC

PROF. DR. GOTTHARD JEDLICKA

Henri de Toulouse-Lautrec

BARNES & NOBLE, INC.

NEW YORK

Publishers • Booksellers • Since 1873

Editor: Anthony Bosman
Translation: Joan Erskine
Published in the United States in 1962
by Barnes & Noble, Inc., 105 Fifth Avenue, New York 3, N.Y.

Great painting during the nineteenth century, in which the French spirit found its purest expression, was either created in Paris or found its starting point in Paris and its surroundings. Yet it is metropolitan only to a slight degree, because in the field of painting one finds the same phenomenon as in sculpture, poetry, and literature in general. In every period in which its creative influence was felt, Paris has created for the whole of France, both consciously and unconsciously. The inexhaustible creativity of the provinces which over the centuries has flowed into Paris has never been stifled by Paris. On the contrary, it has been stimulated there. For centuries, this creativity had become conscious of itself through either accepting or rejecting trends prevailing in Paris.

Throughout the nineteenth century, the provinces, especially those in the South, contributed greatly to Parisian painting. Sometimes these contributions even dominated the scene. From the South of France came Ingres, Daumier, and Cézanne, and each of them not only created great art, but in doing so established an image of the world which cannot be eliminated from the history of French art. Ingres represents, apart from everything to which one can attach the poor label of classicism, the brilliant provincial bourgeoisie of Southern France. With the essence, with the spirit of Paris, his work has little to do. Daumier has the temperament of a man born in a seaport, Marseilles. He has not only retained his Southern French moral and spiritual accent in his creations but in addition has miraculously emphasized it in his artistic creations. Courbet, while painting in Paris, has given lasting expression to the Franche-Comté and its spirit. The inspiration of Paris shows itself in all its power in the impressionist school. None of the "programmatic" impressionists can be regarded as real Parisians: Monet came from Le Havre; Pissarro from the Antilles; Sisley, though born in Paris, remained an Englishman in his art; Renoir came to Paris from Limoges and throughout his life his work remained linked with Limoges and its porcelain painting; Van Gogh came from Holland and lived in Paris only a short time, while he fulfilled his destiny at Arles and St.-Rémy; Cézanne came from Aix-en-Provence and returned there. Toulouse-Lautrec, too, was born in southern France and spent his early childhood there.

Henri de Toulouse-Lautrec (pronounced To-Loose' Low-treck'), who in later life was to sign his works "Lautrec," was born an apparently healthy boy at Albi (near Toulouse in southern France) in 1864. At his birth his parents, who lived separately, agreed to divide his education between themselves. The mother would bring up the child until his sixteenth year; the father would then take over the education of the young man. Henri's father, Count Alphonse de Toulouse-Lautrec II, was an eccentric idler, who delighted in hunting with falcons, followed his whims, and fascinated those about him with his extraordinary pranks. Henri's mother was a good woman to whom her son later referred as a "saint."

At the age of thirteen the boy slipped on a parquet floor and broke his leg. The next year, while traveling, he broke the other. Neither of these fractures healed. His legs stopped growing, while the upper part of his body continued to develop. At the age of fifteen he had become a grotesque dwarf. With his deformed body, Henri had protruding, myopic eyes, thick lips, and a broad, coarse nose, and he also suffered from a speech impediment. As a grown man he once stated that it was

Henri de Toulouse-Lautrec, about 25 years old

his innermost desire to be able to take a daily ride in the Bois de Boulogne as a handsome officer, admired by the elegant ladies of Paris.

Lautrec's work is that of an outsider and a dilettante in the original sense of the word. Ever since he was a child he had made drawings without ever expecting to become a painter. As he loved horses, he took lessons from the painters Princeteau and John Lewis Brown. Later he visited the studio of Cormon, then the Académie Julian. But, above all, he painted and sketched to occupy himself, to while away his time. He probably never thought of earning a living as an artist — his family was wealthy. His friends, too, regarded him as something of an outsider. "Life is beautiful! How beautiful life is!" he often said. His great passion was life — in the streets and in the brothels, on the sports fields and in the bars, at the Moulin-Rouge and in the elegant restaurants, at the circuses and the fairs. Until the last he remained a *"grand seigneur"* with a hobby in which he included those around him.

Again and again the opinion is voiced that Lautrec's subject matter is too circumscribed, limited to Montmartre. Is this correct if one takes his entire work into consideration? The young Lautrec drew hansom cabs and race horses, trotting or galloping; he depicted the people around him, his relatives, workers on the family estate, and his friends — painters, musicians, writers, playwrights, publishers, actors, actresses, singers, and cabaret artists; well-known places of amusement such as the races at Longchamps and Auteuil, the Moulin-Rouge, the circus with its horses and bareback riders, acrobats, and clowns; high and low society frequenting the Parisian cafés and the race tracks, street girls and prostitutes in the brothels, with their clients, among themselves, or alone. He also, toward the end of his life, painted the male nurse at the mental home where he was a patient, and he shows his cousin Gabriel Tapié de Céleyran waiting, seated, to be examined by a doctor. This is merely a brief synopsis of his subjects. There appears to be no painter to whom the description *"fin de siècle"* is so applicable as Lautrec; moreover, he survived the century by only one year. However, the term *"fin de siècle"* has acquired in France an unusually rich significance. Critics who consider such art to be decadent should remember that few other trends in the history of art have shown such creative abundance. Even today Lautrec is too often underestimated. Many art-lovers recognize him as a genius "despite" the subjects he chose to paint. But one must realize that his art has meaning only because of his subjects. The artist is actually the least creative of people because with him the form originates directly from his experience. This form may seem subtle, but in reality the subtlety merely stems from a differentiated experience. The artist, however, whose subjects seem trivial in fact fully reveals the world, because the spectator in looking at his work faces life itself. The world is caught in such a delicate form that the spectator looks past it and instead sees the life which it reveals. Wherever one looks there is life, but on a spiritual plane. Hence that fascinating double effect, that "neither... nor" and "both... and"; the double effect of what is near to life and what is far from it, of the intense expression of the material world and the feverishly spiritual, of abstract vitality and vital abstraction, of the spiritually formal and the formally spiritual, of the abstractedly naïve and the naïvely abstract, of the playfully earnest and the earnestly playful, of the formal in the metaphysical which this genius so brilliantly summarized, independent of any rule or limitation, as he depicted human life and human fate.

At the time when Lautrec worked at Cormon's studio, Japanese art was already known in Paris. Two years before he was born, in 1862, the first Japanese woodcuts were shown at the World Exhibition in London and the first Japanese color prints reached

Paris. The first collectors of these Japanese works were painters themselves: Diaz, Fortuny, Legros, Stevens, Whistler, Manet, Tissot, Fantin-Latour, Monet, Degas, Carolus-Duran, and Bracquemond. They were followed by authors—among them, the Goncourts, Champfleury, Burty, and Zola—publishers, and industrialists. In 1867 Japanese art was represented at the Paris World Exhibition. Four years later an art historian and a collector, Theodore Duret and Cernuschi, made a trip to Japan and returned with woodcuts, bronzes, and books, the latter illustrated by Hokusai and his contemporaries. When, in 1878, Japanese art again made an appearance at the Paris World Exhibition, it no longer caused any real surprise. Finally, in 1883, a group of Parisian collectors put together a retrospective exhibition of Japanese art. In 1891 Edmond de Goncourt wrote the introduction to his book on Utamaro.

Lautrec bought several woodcuts of Harunobu, Kiyonaga, Toyokuni, Utamaro, Hiroshige, and Hokusai, and often gave one of his own works in return.

Among Lautrec's drawings in the collection of Gabriel Tapié de Céleyran is one drawing in India ink which shows how thoroughly Lautrec had studied the Japanese technique. Tapié de Céleyran once showed me the flat ink box which Lautrec used and which he had sent to him from Japan, together with the fine Japanese brush. He also frequently used the brush on his lithographs, as the Japanese do. The influence of Japanese woodcuts is also noticeable in Lautrec's posters, especially in the interlinked lettering and his own signature. Tapié de Céleyran has told me that Lautrec pointed out to him the beauty of the round lettering and crests in Japanese prints and their significance for the composition as a whole. Yeishi signed a series of drawings of courtesans with the drawing of a small rabbit on each sheet. On his "Invitation Alexandre Natanson" Lautrec signed his initials in the center of a black elephant, over

which a kangaroo is leaping. His print "The Dog and the
Parrot", he signed inside the figure of a mole. And yet what a
contrast to Japanese art! Lautrec tries both consciously and
unconsciously to capture the invisible with the brush. He also
tries to seize the fleeting moment and the accidental, that which
happens only once. When he begins to draw, anything can
grow from his brush, anything that is possible in the realm of
his entire human experience. This is often more significant
than the long-premeditated form, clear but lacking in depth.
In his work, expression and experience are mysteriously linked.
Wherever one looks for the one, the other is also there.

With him, experience is the basis of his creations, but what he
creates leads him to deeper experiencing. Suddenly, while
working, he is drawn into the act of creating with all his powers,
as into a maelstrom. During the process of creation the work,
through which he expresses himself, changes constantly. It
becomes richer all the time and that which was given its
apparently definite form is said once again, with deeper meaning
and more beautifully.

Most of Lautrec's paintings which appear to have been painted
quickly are, in fact, the result of long preparation. At all times
and wherever he might be, the artist made notes for paintings.
If he did not have a note book or pad with him, he used wrap-
ping paper, table cloths, the white spaces in a newspaper, book
jackets, or marble table tops. From such notes grew the subjects
and the compositions of his paintings. And even these he
changed several times. His large paintings were done in oil on
canvas or wood. Smaller ones were painted on cardboard,
often without applying a base first, using the color of the cardboard as his basic color. In one and the same painting he used
oil and tempera paints. In his beginning years, he often used
charcoal, later turning to crayon, pencil, and brush. He then
put in the accents with gouache and water color. He seldom

used pastel, and only if he wanted to test the interplay of his colors. Painting a portrait, he seldom worked according to a certain method. He might start at any point that struck him in his model. It might be an eye, it might be the mouth, or the nose. He would paint from this starting point and would make it the center of his composition so that the finished portrait would show a rounded-off composition.

Gabriel Tapié de Céleyran has often told me how Lautrec persuaded people who pleased him as subjects to sit for him. Whenever he met such a person he would go straight to him and, lifting his bowler hat, would address him more or less as follows: "Sir, you would render me an important service if you would sit for me at my studio. The portrait probably won't be like you, but that is of no importance." If the person agreed, the artist would proceed to surround him with attentions. He would be invited to dinner and taken to the theater or to places of amusement. If the model was available for it, the artist would spend whole days with him. Thus he would get to know his model without having to observe him in an obvious way. When the portrait was finished, Lautrec took care to present it properly. He put it under glass if it was done on cardboard and had it framed, always choosing simple frames. He then took a cab, went to see his model, and presented the portrait to him: "Sir, may I thank you again for your kindness. I beg you to accept this portrait from me as a souvenir." This generosity, however, was not always understood.

In his memoirs of Toulouse-Lautrec, Paul Leclerq described how the artist went about painting his portrait. Over a period of one month, Lautrec went to the Avenue Frochot three or four times a week. But one sitting did not last more than a few minutes, only as long as the painter found that the first tension and freshness lasted. Leclerq estimates that Lautrec took in all two or three hours to paint his portrait. As soon as he arrived,

Toulouse-Lautrec working in the garden of Père Forest

he had to sit in a big armchair. The painter then took up his position at the easel, looked sharply at his model through his *pince-nez*, blinked once or twice, took his brush, checked again what he had seen, and then put a few swift strokes on the canvas. While painting he remained outwardly quiet, with only his thick, moist lips in perpetual motion. But all of a sudden he would start singing, off-key, a bawdy song, put down his brush, and say, "Enough work. Weather is too fine." And off they would go together, roaming the streets of Montmartre. Lautrec felt hurt by criticism alleging that he never finished his paintings. His cousin Gabriel told me what the artist had told him in this connection: "All people bore me, after all. They always want me to finish things. But I see them that way and I paint them that way. Look here, it's so easy to finish things. I could easily do you a Bastien-Lepage (a very precise painter)."

At the end of the nineteenth century it was agreed that artistic achievement in the field of lithography had reached a climax in two artists. In the first half of the century it reached a pinnacle in Daumier, and during the second half, in Lautrec. While the former was by and large classified among the romanticists, the latter was often counted among the impressionists—which would be possible only with a number of reservations. Both artists far exceed the confines of any artistic "program," broad as it might be. In both Daumier's and Lautrec's lithographic work all the potentialities of the art of lithography are present. Breadth and intensity, at least to some degree, characterize both Daumier and Lautrec. However, the number of lithographs by Daumier exceeds many times the number created by Lautrec in his short lifetime. Daumier's work is that of an artist who feels that he has a long life before him, Although he drives himself, or is driven, from print to print, he remains essentially unperturbed. Lautrec's lithographs. however, show an artist who, every second of his life, knows that time is running out. The basic character of Daumier's art is therefore epic, while that of Lautrec is dramatic or lyrical.

Daumier not only created series of lithographs, but these could be rearranged into series different from the ones he actually composed, and they could be given different names—for example, "Man and Wife," "Friends," "Enemies," "Good and Evil," "Joys of a Sunday," "Miseries of a Working Day," "Maternal Happiness," "Phases of Life." Lautrec, too, produced series, but the individual prints are not episodes; they exist by themselves. Each of them represents a world, is complete in itself, demands the entire attention of the observer.

Both men's lithographs are works created for a specific occasion. They originated from and were devoted to the demands of the day, and were of an anecdotal character such as one seldom finds in the history of art. But in the anecdotal element these two artists are different. In Daumier's lithographs there is much approximation, while in Lautrec's there is utter precision. In Daumier's work one can find dozens of superficial and even empty prints in which there is nothing of interest but the technique. In Lautrec's lithographs one would vainly search for such examples; each is perfect in its own way. In each, the artist expresses himself as he must, extensively or concisely, generously or sparingly.

Above all, Lautrec has enriched the field of lithography with a new mode of expression—color lithographs. This technique was perfected by him, and his contemporaries Bonnard and Vuillard, though sometimes equaling him, never surpassed him in it. The relationship between one-color and multicolor prints is not always equally pure, but virtually every color lithograph gives the impression that the different colors printed by means of different stones result from logic rather than chance. These color lithographs are among the finest ever created, pure realizations of a unique artistic vision. Some of them are revelations of the moral and intellectual atmosphere of the times and the sensibilities peculiar to the period. They can be festive, feverish, nervous, tender and cruel, beautiful and subtle, full of charm in depicting the perverse, full of elegance in portraying the abject. They are splendid documents — the undying rendering of the fleeting moment.

Never has commercial art found finer expression than in Lautrec's posters. He was the first artist to lend it a genuinely artistic form. He did this by taking it seriously. Many important artists have followed his example, and they have had a decisive and lasting influence on commercial art throughout the first half of the twentieth century. Moreover, after fifty years, the works which Lautrec created in this field have retained all their beauty, richness, and grace. With him, art went out into the street and on walls and billboards proved itself to be genuine art. The man in the street has never been taken more seriously and addressed in a more dignified way than in Lautrec's posters With his poster for the Moulin-Rouge, Lautrec provided an artistic model for the street poster which remained an example for decades. With a complete and intuitive certainty he gives to the street what the street demands. And in addition the poster expresses a purely artistic conception. In the foreground of the Moulin-Rouge poster (p. 25) are "La Goulue" (The Glutton) and "Valentin-le-Désossé" (Valentin the Boneless) both dancing and seen from the side; in the background, visitors to the variety theater. The effect of artificial lighting is achieved through the choice of colors with such skill that even the harshest daylight to which the poster was exposed could not eliminate the impression that the lighting was actually artificial. It is a poster which appears to take into account two ways of viewing: through the eye of a hurrying passer-by and through the gaze of a lingering observer. The passer-by can catch at one single glance what interests him, because it is obvious in the foreground of the poster. But to the observer interested in art, this work remains inexhaustible. The longer he studies it, the more it yields. The entire world of amusement at the Moulin-Rouge is translated into spiritual arabesques in this poster.

The paintings with which Lautrec decorated La Goulue's tent at the Foire du Trône in April, 1895 (pp. 66, 67) became for French painting in the last quarter of the nineteenth century what Watteau's "Enseigne de Gersaint" was for the first quarter of the eighteenth century. In the entire history of Western painting one can find no more brilliant improvisation. Has such a modest commission ever been executed in grander style? It is unthinkable that any of Lautrec's friends would have accepted such a commission—one, moreover, which was unpaid. One of the decorations represents the dancing partners La Goulue and Valentin-le-Désossé, together with an orchestra. The other shows La Goulue dancing with the pianist from the Chat Noir, Tinchant, while the audience consists of Lautrec's friends. The artist himself is among them, seen from the back, a dwarf wearing a bowler hat. He presented both tent decorations to La Goulue, and lost all interest in them. Later they were cut to pieces, and only came together as if by a miracle. Now they are among the most fascinating works in the collection of impressionist paintings in the Jeu de Paume in the Tuileries.

What reveals man's character most strongly? The relationship of man to woman. Time and again Lautrec gave form to this relationship in his paintings, in his drawings, and, above all, in his lithographs, which are a wonderful expression of his hunger for life, which so often appears as hunger for love. He shows the sensual, the spiritual, the intellectual, and the insincere interplay between man and woman, be it in the street, on the stage, or in a variety theater. In Lautrec's work, vulgar lust

17

is confronted with calculating complaisance; hopeless resignation on one side and tense expectation on the other. Always there is an abyss between the partners which is at its deepest whenever they believe themselves to be nearest each other. Whenever he shows the meeting of two people, he makes it look as if these two are destined to be each other's partners for eternity—but that this partnership will be a torment for them. The totality of his work in this respect becomes a succession of moments from life which invariably changes into a dance of the dead. If one looks at a work of this kind one retains the memory, not of a painting, lithograph, or drawing, but of a personal experience. One remembers not merely a work of art, but something that strikes more deeply at the heart.

In the course of his short life Lautrec's color develops and changes enormously. Yet no painter appears to be less concerned with problems of color than he. He starts more or less in the way of the impressionists. He subjects color to the drawing; or, rather, he draws with color. Or again, in his later works he makes the drawing appear less important, resulting in a dominant impression of color and light. This latter effect owes nothing to the painting of his period. He reveals himself at his greatest when he draws with color (in this, his painting allows comparison with that of Van Gogh). The effect of the color is linked to the expressiveness of the drawing. There is no other painter who is less of a painter than he. For that same reason, he creates a most original style of painting, a style of disillusion. His painting is the equivalent in color of the spiritual values he achieves with his drawing.

His drawings go right to the heart of the matter, transforming what he finds into a decorative system of wonderful clarity produced in a casual manner. In the same way his color is spiritual, and in it the visible world is seen as in an X-ray

18

(continued on page 73)

D.03249

picture, showing its spiritual values and inner structure, while retaining its outlines.

Lautrec loved to paint on cardboard of different colors. Sometimes he used smooth canvas as if it were cardboard. His color often has something crayonlike about it. The different colors never form a harmonious whole, but provide a piquant disharmony suggestive of artificiality. In this artificiality, however, they form a decorative and ornamental unity. His painting is, as it were, a synthesis of oils and pastels, of painting and drawing.

There were few places in Paris where Lautrec felt so much at home as in the brothels of the Rue des Moulins, Rue d'Amboise, and Rue Joubert. He compared them with the Japanese geisha houses, of which he had been given detailed information. The paintings he made there were never shown to the public because he feared that they would be misinterpreted. In 1896 he held an exhibition in the Rue Forest. Works which he thought would give offense were hung in two rooms that were separated from the others. The walls of these rooms were covered with strawberry red and green silk, and there were some pieces of yellow furniture. Lautrec kept the key in his pocket, and only his intimate friends were allowed to enter. He refused admission to art dealers who came with the intention of buying, but to his friends who had his confidence he was a gracious host and they always left the rooms with a glass of wine in their hands.

Among the paintings which he withheld from the general public was "The Salon in the Rue des Moulins" (p. 60), now to be seen at the Lautrec Museum at Albi. In these and similar paintings of brothels, a daring theme also used by Constantin Guys before him and by his contemporary Degas has found an expression which one day may be described as classical. This was possible only in Paris and in this form probably only at the end of the nineteenth century. The painting of the salon is the counterpart of Watteau's "Embarquement pour l'Ile de Cythère." In Lautrec's work the mythical island of love has been transformed into a waiting room for venal love. Five of the six women sit on velvet sofas, flanked by walls with huge mirrors. Only one of them is standing, viewed from the back and partly out of the picture. Six women of different ages, different constitutions, different temperaments, and in different stages of physical and spiritual decay. And all, except the one who is only partly shown, are more or less decently dressed. This salesroom of lust is shown with impressive matter-of-factness. Here is no hidden leer, no ambiguity, but the consummate tact which is characteristic of Lautrec. The warm colors which are dominant in this room are the equivalent in color of what passes here for love.

Lautrec is a Parisian. His work catches the atmosphere peculiar to a metropolis. It gives shape, as the work of no other artist has done, to the rhythm of the city, its speed, its fever, its quick perception. His work, down to individual sketches, has drawn into its orbit the monstrous decay of life in a big city, especially in the Montmartre of Paris. The hectic quality of life, which appears to escape any attempt at definition, is given form in ever-changing curves and arabesques. In representing artificiality, fullness and emptiness, naïveté and sophistication, his work has become pure and great art.

In his work, a woman's make-up—the significance of which, in the nineteenth century, only Baudelaire realized as deeply as Lautrec—appears as the expression of a myth based on vitality itself, as a dreamlike intensification of beauty. It appears as an effort on the part of the woman to retain her power of turning heads, offering temptation, giving happiness. With all this, Lautrec not only sees life, he sees through it. For that reason he does not limit himself to mere representation of the heavily

Henri de Toulouse-Lautrec, at the age of 30 years

made-up woman, but in so doing he shows the contrast between reality and appearance, between everyday life and dreams.

Lautrec's touch, whether in painting, lithography, or sketching, is the most sensitive of nineteenth-century French art. Many important artists want their touch to express all, but they merely indicate; Lautrec contents himself with indicating and in so doing is wonderfully expressive, because to him, his art is everything. As soon as he starts to paint or sketch he expresses feelings and experiences but, above all, experiences. He does this in a personal way, so spontaneous and individual, so without any preconceived intention, that one could not possibly mistake his work for that of another. With no other artist does one so easily forget the style and see only what is expressed, because the style immediately reveals the essence.

He paints in such a deceptively casual manner that one forgets what with Ingres, Daumier, Delacroix, Degas, and Manet one very seldom forgets—that sketching is a trade which one has to learn and relearn. With Lautrec it seems part of his nature, although impressions can be misleading. Whenever a work of art bursts with life, this has its origin in the artist's power of expression, because the formless will never produce an artistic effect. Lautrec's work radiates so much life because it contains his entire being—his feelings, his spirit, his senses, and his experiences. In his art, whether he was sketching, creating lithographs, or painting, he used himself to the limit.

His whole complicated personality, liberated from all inhibitions and obstacles, flows into his brush, producing that graphically visible vibration which reveals itself in a differentiated curve. In this one great curve, subsidiary curves appear, overlapping each other and finally resolving themselves into the one curve. In this way, Lautrec gives us his view of the totality of life. His curves represent the seismographic script of the most diverse simultaneous emotions.

76

At the end of the nineteenth century Lautrec is the only artist in France in whose work man stands in the center, man only. The "programmatic" impressionists had banned man from their subject world. Renoir in his late works had depersonalized him; for the old Degas, he no longer existed as an individual; in Cézanne's portraits he loses more and more of his individuality. Only in Lautrec's artistic creations is the human individual naturally and totally present. Lautrec is the only one among the great painters who does not divorce man from his fate. He not only puts him in the center of his work but with him also his spiritual and moral destiny. What does it matter that in many cases the subject stands on the edge of human society? Does not every human being stand there with at least a part of his personality? That is what Lautrec would seem to say. This deep humanity, to which nothing human remains alien makes Lautrec's work unique.

Lautrec is forever looking inward and outward at the same time, encompassing light and dark. Each painting, lithograph, and sketch grows from a spiritual content which determines the smallest detail and which remains the unvarying aim of the work. His forms sometimes are produced with such subtle brushstrokes that these disappear when looked at sharply, like the mist of breath on a windowpane. His forms are always experiences. He depicted life as he observed it. He did not attempt to gloss over depravity and vice, but portrayed them accurately.

Lautrec's lifespan was three dozen years, of which only half was taken up by his work as an artist. His work is great because each detail originated from an inner necessity, because he did only what his inner self forced him to do, and while creating he forged his own destiny.

LIST OF ILLUSTRATIONS

19 THE COUNTESS A. DE TOULOUSE-LAUTREC (the artist's mother)
1887; oil; $21\frac{1}{4} \times 17\frac{3}{4}$ in.; Musée d'Albi, France

20 YOUNG WOMAN IN THE STUDIO OF THE ARTIST
1888; gouache; $29\frac{1}{2} \times 19\frac{3}{4}$ in.; Kunsthalle, Bremen

21 MLLE. DIHAU AT THE PIANO (a singer, a relative of Lautrec)
1890; oil; $26\frac{3}{4} \times 19\frac{1}{4}$ in.; Musée d'Albi, France

22 YOUNG WOMAN IN A STUDIO
1888; oil; $32\frac{1}{4} \times 24$ in.; Museum of Fine Arts, Boston

23 M. HENRI DIHAU (bass at the Paris Opera)
1891; oil; $21\frac{3}{4} \times 17\frac{3}{4}$ in.; Musée d'Albi, France

24 AT THE MOULIN-ROUGE
1892; oil; $47\frac{1}{2} \times 55\frac{1}{4}$ in.; Art Institute of Chicago

25 LA GOULUE AND VALENTIN-LE-DÉSOSSÉ AT THE MOULIN-ROUGE
1891; lithograph (poster); $76\frac{1}{2} \times 48$ in.

26 THE FIRST MAILLOT
1890; oil; 23×17 in.; Goldschmidt collection, Berlin

27 JANE AVRIL DANCING IN THE MOULIN-ROUGE (The dancer Jane
Avril was the daughter of a demimondaine and an Italian
nobleman. She danced with La Goulue the *"quadrille naturaliste."* The *"quadrille naturaliste"* was derived from the cancan,
which had gone out of fashion after the war of 1870 and was
brought to a new and more sensational life by La Goulue
and Valentin-le-Désossé about 1890.)
1892; thinned oil; $33\frac{1}{4} \times 17\frac{1}{4}$ in.; Louvre, Paris

28 THE PHOTOGRAPHER GEORGES HENRI MANUEL in Lautrec's
studio
1891; oil; $33 \times 13\frac{1}{4}$ in.; private collection

29 JANE AVRIL LEAVING THE MOULIN-ROUGE
1892; oil; 34 × 25½ in.; Wadsworth Atheneum, Hartford, Conn.

30 THE ENGLISHMAN AT THE MOULIN-ROUGE
1892; color lithograph; 18½ × 14½ in.

31 ARISTIDE BRUANT AT THE ELDORADO (Bruant, who started his cabaret Le Mirliton in 1885, was a famous *chansonnier*, who abused his visitors rudely between songs and mocked them with the slogan "All visitors are pigs.")
1892; lithograph (poster); 59 × 39½ in.

32 AT THE NOUVEAU CIRQUE: FIVE STUFFED SHIRTS
1891; design for a poster, which was never produced; 23¾ × 16¾ in.; Museum of Art, Philadelphia

33 JANE AVRIL AT THE JARDIN DE PARIS
1893; color lithograph (poster); 51 × 37⅜ in.

34 WALTZING WOMEN AT THE MOULIN-ROUGE
1892; oil; 32 × 31 in.; Museum of Modern Art, Prague

35 LOUIS PASCAL (cousin of Lautrec)
1893; oil; 30¾ × 20¾ in.; Musée d'Albi, France

36 YVETTE GUILBERT BOWING TO THE PUBLIC
1894; charcoal and thinned oil; 18¾ × 9¾ in.; Musée d'Albi, France

37 JANE AVRIL LEAVING THE MOULIN-ROUGE AND PUTTING ON HER GLOVES
1892; pastel and oil on millboard; 40 × 22 in.; Courtauld Institute of Art, London (by permission of the Home House Trustees)

38 WOMAN WITH BLACK FUR
1892; oil; 21 × 17 in.; Louvre, Paris

39 THE COIFFURE
1891; oil; 17 × 11¾ in.; Eugène Blot collection, Paris

40 THE COIFFURE
November, 1893; lithograph for the program of the play
Une Faillite in the Théâtre Libre; 12½ × 9½ in.

41 THE MODISTE RENÉE VERT
1893; lithograph; 14¼ × 13¾ in.

42 MME. DE GORTZIKOFF (the only portrait which Lautrec made
on commission)
1893; oil; 30 × 20 in.; private collection

43 ALFRED LA GUIGNE AT THE BAR
1894; oil; 33½ × 24¾ in.; private collection

44 LELOIR AND MORENO, in Molière's *Les Femmes savantes*
September, 1893; lithograph; 14¾ × 10¼ in.

45 CAUDIEUX (comedian of the Petit-Casino)
December, 1893; lithograph from the series "Le Café-
Concert"; 10¾ × 9½ in.

46 LUGNÉ POE AND MLLE. BALDY in Beaubourg's play *L'Image*
in L'Oeuvre Théâtre
March, 1894; lithograph; 12¼ × 9 in.

47 THE ACTRESS BRANDES AND THE ACTOR LELOIR in the play
Cabotins
February, 1894; lithograph; 15¾ × 11¾ in.

48 CARNIVAL
March, 1894; lithograph; 10¼ × 8 in.

49 THE CANAPÉ (one of the numerous studies for "The Salon
in the Rue des Moulins")
1894-95; thinned oil; 23½ × 31½ in.; Museu de Arte, São
Paulo

50 LA GOULUE DANCING WITH VALENTIN-LE-DÉSOSSÉ the quadrille
at the Moulin-Rouge. (Between 1890 and 1895 La Goulue
was the star of the Moulin-Rouge. Her proper name was
Louise Weber. She was an Alsatian laundress who was discov-
ered by a Paris impresario in 1886. She was good-looking,
but vulgar, haughty, and coarse. Her partner, Valentin-le-
Désossé, was the owner of a small café, who came to dance
in the Moulin-Rouge in the evenings as a pastime.)
1894; lithograph; $11\frac{3}{4} \times 9$ in.

51 YVETTE GUILBERT AS AN ENGLISHWOMAN (one of 16 lithographs dedicated to the famous performer)
$10\frac{1}{2} \times 7$ in.

52 THE ACTRESS MARCELLE LENDER
1895; color lithograph; $12\frac{3}{4} \times 9\frac{1}{2}$ in.

53 MISS MAY BELFORT (Irish singer)
1895; oil; $31\frac{1}{2} \times 23\frac{3}{4}$ in.; Bernheim-Jeune collection, Paris

54 AT PICTON'S BAR IN THE RUE SCRIBE NUMBER 4
1896; lithograph; $11\frac{3}{4} \times 9$ in.

55 GABRIEL TAPIÉ DE CÉLEYRAN in the lounge of the Comédie
Française (cousin of Lautrec; they were brought up together
as children; he studied medicine and was an inseparable
companion to the artist on his expeditions through Paris at
night)
1894; oil; $43\frac{1}{4} \times 22$ in.; Musée d'Albi, France

56 THE FAINT
1899; lithograph

57 THE LAUNDRYMAN OF THE BROTHEL
1894; oil; $26\frac{1}{2} \times 17\frac{3}{4}$ in.; Musée d'Albi, France

58 THE HORSEWOMAN AND THE DOG
1899; lithograph; $10\frac{3}{4} \times 9\frac{1}{4}$ in.

59 NAPOLEON I ON HORSEBACK
September, 1895; color lithograph (poster, designed for a competition on the subject of Napoleon but rejected); 23¼ × 17¾ in.

60 THE SALON IN THE RUE DES MOULINS
1894-95; oil; 43¼ × 47¼ in.; Musée d'Albi, France

61 PAUL LECLERQ (writer and founder of the *Revue Blanche*, in which several lithographs of Lautrec were published)
1897; oil; 21¼ × 25¼ in.; Louvre, Paris

62 INVITATION TO JOIN IN A GLASS OF MILK ("Henri de Toulouse-Lautrec will be very honored if you will accept a glass of milk on Saturday, May 15, at about half-past three in the afternoon.")
1900; lithograph; 10½ × 8 in.

63 MISS DOLLY (English barmaid at the cabaret Du Star, Le Havre)
1899; oil; 16 × 12½ in.; Musée d'Albi, France

64 IN THE BOIS DE BOULOGNE
1901; oil; private collection

65 AT THE RACES
1899; oil; 17¾ × 20¾ in.; Musée d'Albi, France

66 THE DANCE OF LA GOULUE AND VALENTIN-LE-DÉSOSSÉ (Decoration on the right front-cloth of the tent of La Goulue at the Foire du Trône. When La Goulue (The Glutton) became too fat to perform in the cabarets, she became a belly-dancer at the fair.)
1895; oil; 118 × 118 in.; Musée de l'Impressionisme, Paris

67 THE DANCE OF LA GOULUE OF "LES ALMÉES." (left front-cloth of the tent described above)
1895; oil; 118 × 118 in.; Musée de l'Impressionisme, Paris

68 MLLE. COCYTE of the opera at Bordeaux, in *La Belle Hélène*
December, 1900; black crayon; 13¼ × 9½ in.; private collection

69 PRIVATE ROOM IN THE RESTAURANT LE RAT MORT (portrait
of the demimondaine Lucy Jourdan)
1899; oil on canvas; 21½ × 17¾ in.; Courtauld Institute of
Art, London (by permission of the Home House Trustees)

70 THE CHESTNUT-SELLER (the last work of Lautrec before he
died on September 9, 1901)
April, 1901; lithograph; 10¼ × 6¾ in.

71 THE MODISTE
1900; oil; 24 × 19½ in.; Musée d'Albi, France

72 MME. POUPOULE AT HER TOILETTE
1900; oil; 23½ × 19¼ in.; Musée d'Albi, France